LiZARDs
Weird and Wonderful

by **MARGERY FACKLAM**   Illustrated by **ALAN MALE**

LITTLE, BROWN AND COMPANY

New York ✍ An AOL Time Warner Company

Lizards are acrobats. They leap and strut and swim. They can glide through the air, run across water on their hind legs, or walk upside down on the ceiling.

Lizards are look-alikes. Some look like alligators, others like snakes, and some look like make-believe dragons. Many small lizards are mistaken for salamanders, but they are very different animals.

Salamanders are amphibians with smooth, moist skin. Like all amphibians, they lay their jelly-covered eggs in water. When the eggs hatch, the babies look nothing like their parents. They breathe through gills until they change into land animals that breathe with lungs. A salamander has no claws on its toes, and it has no eardrums.

Lizards are reptiles. They breathe with lungs, and they are covered with scales. Some scales are like little beads or bumps and others overlap like shingles on a roof. Most lizards shed their skin in bits and pieces, but smooth lizards called skinks shed their skin in one piece.

The female lizards lay their eggs on land. When the babies hatch from the leathery eggs, they look like miniature adults. Lizards have claws on their five toes. Most lizards have eyelids that open and close, and just behind their eyes, all lizards have two round spots, which are their eardrums.

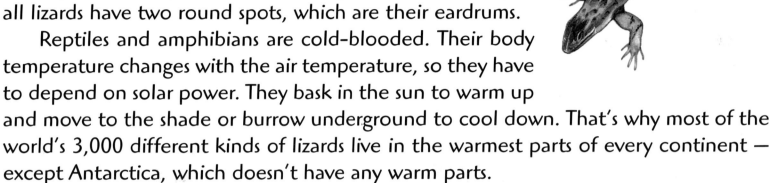

Reptiles and amphibians are cold-blooded. Their body temperature changes with the air temperature, so they have to depend on solar power. They bask in the sun to warm up and move to the shade or burrow underground to cool down. That's why most of the world's 3,000 different kinds of lizards live in the warmest parts of every continent — except Antarctica, which doesn't have any warm parts.

The largest lizard is ten feet long, but the smallest could sit on a matchstick. A few lizards may be fierce, but most are as harmless as a worm. Only one kind is armed with venom.

The science of studying reptiles and amphibians is called *herpetology*. *Herpe* is a Greek word that means "creeping things," and *-ology* means the "study of." Herpetologists are the scientists who study these "creeping things," including the amazing lizards you'll find on these pages.

KOMODO DRAGON

There's one kind of monitor you wouldn't want patrolling the halls of your school, because it's a lizard big enough and strong enough to kill a horse!

The Komodo dragon belongs to the family of monitor lizards that live in Africa, Asia, and Australia. It is the largest lizard in the world, and the only one that lives in a national park that was made for its protection. The park on Komodo Island in the South Pacific Ocean is part of Indonesia.

One scientist described the dragon's skin as "loose and a little baggy, a comfortable fit for an athlete." As a powerful runner, a full-grown, 300-pound, ten-foot-long Komodo dragon is an athlete of sorts. Its long, tough tail can knock down almost any prey, and its razor-sharp three-inch claws can rip through the tough hide of a water buffalo. After a meal the size of a buffalo, a dragon may have to rest for a week, but it is also content to feed on smaller animals, dead or alive.

Komodos are almost a foot long when they hatch from their eggs. At first they live in trees, out of reach of hungry predators, especially grown-up dragons. When they are too big to live in trees, young komodos become hunters and scavengers on the ground, plodding along on feet as big as a bear's. Their head swings from side to side on a long neck, which is very flexible because it has nine neck bones. (Giraffes have only seven, and so do we.)

A Komodo's forked tongue constantly slips in and out, tasting and smelling the air. The two tips of the tongue fit perfectly into two small holes in the roof of its mouth, where snakes and lizards have a kind of "supernose" called Jacobson's organ that tells them what they taste and smell.

At one time, tourists on Komodo Island could watch from bleachers as the huge lizards fed on dead goats. But after several visitors were attacked because they got too close to the hungry dragons, the park rangers stopped that kind of tourist attraction.

CHAMELEON

"What happened to the chameleon that sat on a man's plaid shirt?"

"It went crazy trying to match the pattern!"

That's an old joke, and lucky for chameleons, it's not true. They do not change color just to blend in with their background. Experiments have proved that a chameleon's color changes when it is sick, or startled by a predator, or when there is a sudden change in air temperature or light. A change in color can also send a message. When a male panther chameleon sees a female, his body quickly turns from dull green to bright yellow with black stripes and red spots. That tells the female, "I want to be your mate."

Eighty-five kinds of chameleons, with names such as fork-nose, flap-neck, and elephant ear, live in Africa, Madagascar, and India. The smallest is no bigger than your thumb, and the biggest is two feet long. All of them are goofy-looking, with helmet-heads and leaf-shaped bodies that are flattened sideways, as though they've been smacked between two giant hands. Five stubby toes sprout from the ankles of their sticklike legs. A clump of two toes on one side and three on the other can clamp on a branch like a pair of tongs. Their long flexible tail is *prehensile*. That means it's made for hanging on. But each species of chameleon has different colors, patterns, flaps, fringes, or horns.

Chameleons can't open or close their eyes, but they have excellent vision. Their scaly eyelids are joined together into a dome shape, with only a peephole to see through. One eye can look up while the other swivels down, or one forward and the other back, or both eyes can focus together.

A chameleon moves slower than a slug, but its extremely long tongue shoots out faster than you can blink. In less than half a second, the biggest chameleons can catch prey as heavy as a bird on the tip of their sticky tongue and pull it back into their mouth. This is equal to a 150-pound man lifting a 22-pound weight on his tongue!

ANOLE

Almost everyone in North America knows the little green anole. In the south, people see them in backyards. People in the north see them in zoos, or in pet stores, where they are sold as American chameleons. Anoles, the smallest members of the iguana family, are not real chameleons. They do change color, but only to different shades of brown or green, depending on the temperature, the amount of light, or the anole's activity.

Years ago, live anoles were sold as jewelry. A tiny collar around the anole's neck was attached to a miniature leash that could be looped around a button on a woman's coat. That was cruel, and it's not allowed anymore. But anoles are still sold as pets. If you have one, remember that an anole won't drink from a water bottle or a dish. It laps up drops of water on leaves.

Like many animals, lizards spend their lives in a specific area or territory. A naturalist who shared his patio with a male anole liked to watch this lizard defend his territory from other males. One day the man put a mirror against the wall to see what would happen. The first time the anole saw himself in the mirror, he stopped and stared at this "other" male. He flared out the red pouch under his chin. So did the male in the mirror, but the real anole didn't back down. He straightened his legs and raised his body to look bigger and more fierce. So did his image. For an hour and a half the anole strutted up and down, bobbing his head until he was worn out. He would run away for a while, but when he came back, this other anole was still there, threatening his territory. He did this for six weeks! Once he even looked behind the mirror, and several times he tried to bite his own image. If the real anole had chased the other male away, his skin would be bright green. If he had backed down, his skin would turn dull brown.

Scientists were interested in this anole's adventure because it meant the lizard could remember for a long time that the other anole was still waiting to steal his territory.

HORNED LIZARD

Why was this lizard once called a toad? Maybe it's because it is brown and round, and its bumpy back looks like a toad's warty skin. It also snaps up insects and burrows into the ground like a toad. At one time, these little lizards were so popular as pets that they were in danger of becoming extinct. Now they are protected by laws that prevent people from taking them home as souvenirs from the Grand Canyon or buying them in pet stores. And now they are called horned lizards.

Seven different kinds of horned lizards live in the United States and Mexico, and one of them, the short-horned lizard, also lives in western Canada. Nights are cold in the desert, so horned lizards bury themselves in the soil at night to keep warm. They also sleep through winter. Most hibernating animals fill up on food before their winter sleep, but horned lizards stop eating. Without the warmth of the sun, they don't have enough energy to digest hard-shelled insects. Food left in their stomachs during hibernation would rot and make them sick.

Horned lizards' favorite fast-food place is an anthill, but some of them are fussy eaters. Texas horned lizards eat only harvester ants. In the same habitat, roundtail horned lizards eat only honeypot ants — as many as 70 to 100 a day. A small lizard can live for a whole month on the amount of food one small, insect-eating bird needs for only one day.

Horned lizards have several ways to protect themselves from hawks, roadrunners, coyotes, and other predators. They can hide. Pressed to the ground, flat as a pancake, they disappear against the sand. They can stand their ground and bluff, or puff up to look bigger, or run away. But when they squirt a fine stream of blood from their eyes, even the biggest predators, including people, are surprised enough to back off. No other animal has this amazing secret weapon.

CHUCKWALLA

Who would ever guess that a lizard as tough and sturdy as the chuckwalla would love flowers, especially yellow blossoms? In zoos, chuckwallas can be coaxed to eat mealworms, but in the wild they are vegetarians. When a park ranger in the Grand Canyon studied the contents of one chuckwalla's stomach, he found 118 flower heads from the indigo bush, mallow plant, prickly pear cactus, and creosote bush, which this lizard had eaten for breakfast.

Chuckwallas are part of the iguana family. Their name came from Spanish settlers who called them *chacahuala*. These twelve-inch lizards live on the rocky ledges of America's southwest deserts, where their rusty brown scales blend into the background. Young chuckwallas have bands of brown on their tails, but old ones really look old because their backs and tails turn dusty white.

Raymond Ditmars, who was a famous herpetologist, described the way this chunky lizard runs as "a rapid waddle." Even so, a chuckwalla can often escape a hungry coyote, hawk, or other predator. Its secret weapon is its loose, saggy skin. A chuckwalla's territory might be more than an acre, but the lizard knows every rock and crevice in it. At the first shadow of a hawk overhead, a chuckwalla scrambles into the nearest crack in the rocks. As it grips the rock with its claws, it gulps air to fill up its lungs. The loose skin tightens around its puffed-up body until the chuckwalla is stuck so firmly in the crack that most predators can't get it out.

Chuckwallas have often saved the lives of people who were stranded for days under the hot desert sun without food or water. Prospectors and other desert travelers probably learned from the Native Americans how to poke a puffed-up chuckwalla with a sharp stick to deflate it so it can be pulled free. Some say a chuckwalla roasted over an open fire is very tasty and tender, because it has eaten flowers.

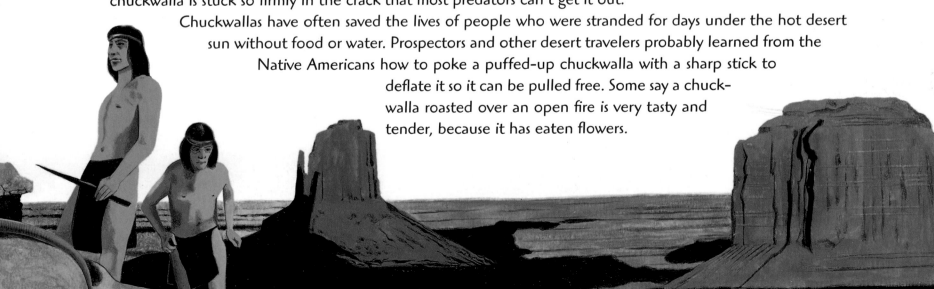

MARINE IGUANA

Ocean waves crash over a lava rock cliff, where a mob of marine iguanas wait for the morning sun to warm them. Now and then the pug-nosed lizards snort salty seawater from their nostrils. Otherwise they seldom move, not even when the Sally Lightfoot crabs scurry over them to eat bits of their shedding skin. They pay no attention to the tourists who crowd close enough to take pictures. These four-foot-long lizards are used to the thousands of people who visit the Galapagos Islands on the equator, 600 miles off the coast of South America.

In 1835, before Charles Darwin became one of the world's most famous scientists, he sailed to the Galapagos. When he saw a marine iguana, he wrote in his journal, "It is a hideous looking creature of a dirty black colour, stupid and sluggish in its movements."

He must have written that before he saw them dive into the sea, because these clumsy-looking iguanas are graceful swimmers. They are the only lizards that go into the ocean to feed on algae. With their strong tails moving from side to side in powerful strokes, they can cruise underwater for almost an hour. When they stop to bite off chunks of algae and seaweed, they hang on to rocks with their long, sharp claws.

Except for hungry sharks that might grab one of them in the water now and then, marine iguanas have few enemies. The Galapagos Islands are protected as a national park of Ecuador. No guns are allowed. It is against the law to kill or hurt an animal. But in January, 2001, the most dangerous enemy of all made a sneak attack. A small freighter loaded with 240,000 gallons of diesel oil hit a reef. Oil spilled out of the ship's damaged hull. It covered the water and oozed toward shore. An oil slick is a silent, sneaky enemy that marine animals can't fight or learn to avoid. Iguanas, sea lions, birds, and fish choke on it and drown in it. People caused the problem, but people can fix it.

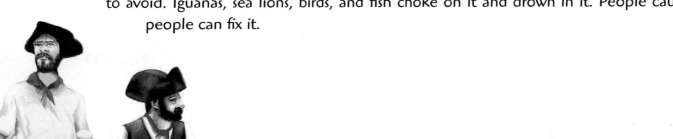

BASILISK

If we gave prizes for different kinds of iguanas, the common green iguana might win first place as the best pet, or even the most delicious lizard. In Central and South America green iguanas are called *gallina de palo,* or "chicken of the tree," because they are so good to eat. The big land iguanas from the Galapagos Islands might get a prize for being tough, because they eat the fruit of cactus, even the prickly parts. The marine iguanas might be named best swimmers. But there would be no argument about first prize for weirdest. That would go to the basilisks.

In ancient times, people in Greece and Rome told stories about a mythical reptile they called the basilisk. It was said to have the head and legs of a bird and a long, snakelike tail. They believed it could destroy any living thing just by looking at it or breathing on it. A basilisk could even knock a man off a horse with its fearful breath!

Over the next several centuries, the story grew. People began to believe that if a basilisk heard a cock crow, it would die. So travelers carried roosters with them. When the first voyagers from Europe landed in Central and South America, they probably wished they'd brought more roosters. They must have been convinced of the basilisk's magic power when they saw these small iguanas that had the head and legs of a bird and the long, scaly tail of a snake.

In South America and Panama, basilisks are called *paso-rios,* the river-crossers, or "the Jesus beasts," because they walk on water. Basilisks like to live in trees near water, so that at the first sign of danger, they can drop from a branch to the water below. They can run on top of the water because they are fast, and their long, fringed toes keep them from sinking until they slow down. With their tail held high for balance, and their short front legs pumping like the arms of a human runner, these odd little iguanas look like miniature dinosaurs — or animals right out of an ancient myth.

FENCE LIZARD

The way fence lizards dart around, it's no wonder that people used to call them "swifts." The fence lizard is one of a big group of spiny lizards. All of them are rough as pinecones, because their scales are *keeled.* The ridge on the bottom of a boat is called the keel, and that's what each scale has — a raised ridge like the keel of a boat.

All across the United States, except where the winters are too harsh, fence lizards live in gardens and woodlots. They are good to have around, because they eat so many insects and spiders, but you have to be as patient as a bird-watcher to see one. If you do catch a glimpse of a fence lizard, it's likely to be sunning itself on a fence or darting up a tree. When it sees you, it will "freeze." It will sit so still that it seems to disappear against the bark. Reach for it, and it will shoot around the far side of the tree trunk and wait. Every time you make a grab for it, the fence lizard dashes around to the other side, a little higher each time. When you think you've caught it, you're likely to have only its tail in your hand.

A lizard's tail doesn't drop off just any old time. The lizard uses it as a way to escape. There are lines called "fracture planes" in the center of several of the lizard's vertebrae (backbones) where the tail breaks easily. Special muscles around these bones allow the tail to separate from the lizard's body when it is grabbed, and other muscles squeeze the blood vessels to stop the wound from bleeding. Muscles in the broken-off tail keep it wiggling on the ground for several seconds, which gives the lizard time to escape while the predator watches the old tail twitch. A new tail begins to grow right away, but it's never as long and graceful as the first one, and it has no bones. The new tail is supported by a rod of softer tissue called *cartilage,* which is the bendy kind of tissue that gives an ear its shape. But a short, stumpy tail is not a bad trade-off for a safe escape.

GLASS SNAKE

If ever an animal had the wrong name, it is the glass snake. It is not a snake, and it's certainly not made of glass. This lizard without legs is easy to mistake for a snake, until it blinks. Snakes can't blink because they don't have eyelids. Snakes also don't have eardrums or a long groove running down each side, as a glass snake does. The grooves give this lizard's body room to stretch after a big meal, and space for the female's eggs to grow inside her body. If a glass snake flipped over, you'd see that its belly is covered with many rows of small scales. A snake's belly has only one line of single, wide scales called *scutes.*

Glass snakes live in meadows and woodlands from Lake Michigan to states eastward and south to Mexico. Full-grown glass snakes, three feet long, ought to be easy to find in these habitats, but they're usually underground or hidden in woodpiles looking for a juicy meal of earthworms, slugs, or mice. You won't find a glass snake in a tree because it can't climb, and even when it crawls on the ground it doesn't slither gracefully like a snake because the tough, bony plates under its skin make it stiff.

Old stories say a glass snake breaks into splinters if you pick it up. Others call it a "joint snake" that somehow joins the pieces of its broken tail together again, good as new. But these stories are not true.

A snake's tail is only a few inches long. The tail of a glass snake is more than twice as long as the rest of its body. It is unpleasant to pick up a glass snake because of the way it thrashes and twists until its tail breaks. The tail doesn't shatter into little splinters, but it is so long and brittle that it does come apart in several pieces. The glass snake's new tail is much shorter than the old one, and the tip of it is as hard and pointed as a thorn. Some people call it a stinger, but that's just another of those old tales people like to tell.

GECKO

A thousand different kinds of geckos live in deserts, rain forests, and cities in tropical climates. Most geckos are nocturnal, which means they are active at night. They have eyes like a cat, with vertical pupils. In tropical countries, geckos live in almost every house. These small, harmless lizards aren't pets. They are welcome guests, free to come and go. As night falls, geckos scurry up walls and race across ceilings, eating insects, especially cockroaches. The skin of some geckos is so thin, you can almost see through it. They look like tiny ghosts, but they sound like birds. Geckos are the only lizards that "sing." Some of their clicks and chirps sound like "Geck-o, geck-o." These sounds gave them their name.

Geckos that run around during the day have large, round eyes. Instead of eyelids, geckos have clear, transparent eye covers, which they can clean with a swipe of their fleshy tongue. When the eye covers are shed along with the old skin, there are fresh ones already in place.

How can a gecko stick to a ceiling or run up a wall so easily? There are no suction cups or glue on a gecko's feet. Such stickiness would prevent a gecko from moving fast enough to catch insects. Each step would take too much energy to pull free. Some scientists, who call themselves the Gecko Team, looked at gecko toes under a powerful electron microscope. They saw thousands of leaves of very thin tissue on each toe. Each leaf had hundreds of thousands of hairlike strands, and each strand had hundreds of thousands of tiny, flat tips. The scientists learned that each flat tip peels back, one after another, so easily that the gecko can raise its foot very fast. The Gecko Team's discovery could lead to inventions such as stronger adhesive tape that can be used many times, or gecko tape for attaching equipment to space stations. And imagine gecko gloves and shoes that would let rock climbers or robots move around like Spider-Man.

FIVE-LINED SKINK

Blue is a popular color for lizards, especially skinks. A big lizard called the blue-tongue skink lives in Australia, and many of the smaller skinks in North America wear a blue spot under the chin or blue splotches on their sides like a vest. When they are young, almost all the North American skinks have bright blue tails that break off very easily. You may not want to catch a skink, because it will probably try to bite you, and you'll only end up with its tail in your hand, anyway.

Skinks are sleek lizards with smooth, shiny scales. The five-lined skink is only five or six inches from head to tail, but it's a fighter, especially when it's hunting for wasps or yellow jackets. One herpetologist watched a skink grab a wasp's nest in its jaws and shake it and thrash it around until it broke apart. When the young wasps dropped out, the skink gobbled them up. The adult wasps swarmed around trying to sting the lizard, but their stingers couldn't get through the skink's tough scales. Another five-lined skink was seen raiding twenty wasps' nests and twelve yellow jackets' nests in two weeks.

As five-lined skinks get old, their stripes fade and their blue tails turn brown, but the male's head swells up and becomes bright red. Scientists used to think a red-headed, five-lined skink was an entirely different kind of lizard. In some parts of the country, people thought it was poisonous, so they called it a "scorpion lizard."

After a female skink lays her eggs, she doesn't leave them, as most other lizards do. She curls her body around the eggs and guards them until they hatch, but she pays no attention to the new baby skinks. She doesn't really need to, because all reptile babies are *precocious* (prih-KOH-shus). That means they are born knowing how to take care of themselves. All the information they need is coded in their genes. It's called "instinct."

GILA MONSTER (pronounced HEE-la)

Most descriptions of the Gila monster call this lizard ugly, clumsy, or disgusting. But what other animal looks like it's made of beautiful, colored beads? The Gila monster's round scales are arranged in splotches of black and patches of pink and orange. Its close cousin, the Mexican beaded lizard, is black and yellow. The bead pattern is different on each lizard, just as the pattern of stripes is different on each zebra.

Maybe the nasty descriptions of these beaded lizards are meant to scare people away, and that's a good idea, because they are the only lizards in the world that have venom. They don't have fangs like a poisonous snake; when they bite, the venom oozes from a gland on their lower jaw into the wound made by their sharp teeth. A beaded lizard hangs on like a bull dog and chews to help spread the venom. Sometimes their jaws have to be pried apart to make them let go.

Full-grown Gila monsters are two feet long. They are the largest lizards in the United States and are so rare now that they are protected by laws to save them from extinction. They live in the Sonoran Desert of America's southwest and northern Mexico, where days can get hot enough to bake a cold-blooded reptile, but nights are cold. So these lizards spend most of their lives underground in tunnels they dig with their long claws, or in burrows they borrow from pack rats and other animals. They hibernate from November to January or February. They also *estivate*, which means they sleep through the heat of summer.

A Gila monster can survive for months without food if it has enough fat stored in its tail. After a long sleep, its tail is skinny. It is hungry and ready to hunt. Its tongue flicks in and out, tasting and smelling the air, looking for small animals or a nest of eggs. Its jaws can crack an egg as easily as we pop bubble gum, and with its thick tongue, a Gila monster laps up a favorite meal.

FLYING DRAGON

In the rain forests of Indonesia and the Philippines, there's a lizard that might make you think of Superman. It is called the flying dragon, but its scientific name, *Draco volans*, is a great name for a lizard. And it's fun to say.

When a Draco is resting on a tree, it looks so much like the bark that you'd hardly notice it unless it nodded its head or spread the yellow sac under its chin. Its scrawny body is only seven or eight inches long, but its thin tail adds another four or five inches. With loose, saggy skin folded along its sides, Draco isn't very pretty. It seems to be wearing an oversize, hand-me-down coat.

But when Draco suddenly runs a few steps and leaps from the tree, those folds of skin turn into a spectacular colored cape. Draco floats through the air, then lands easily on a tree fifty or sixty feet away. The cape is a flap of skin attached to several pairs of long ribs. When these ribs are spread and the skin stretches between its front and back legs, Draco looks like a huge, black-and-orange butterfly.

Life at the top of a 400-foot tree in a rain forest can be dangerous for any small creature. Even an animal with a cape can slip and tumble head over tail before it has a chance to get its balance and spread its "wings." But Draco is lucky. Thorny antiskid scales on the underside of its tail grip the bark like cleats on a mountain climber's boots.

The female Dracos have to come down to the ground to lay their eggs. Otherwise, flying dragons spend their lives in the upper layers of the forest called the "canopy," where trees overlap to form a roof of leaves. There's always enough to eat. Draco's favorite food is a big helping of tree ants, but there are so many different kinds of insects and spiders to choose from in a rain forest that scientists haven't even named them all yet.

HOW TO TELL THE DIFFERENCE — OR TRY TO

SNAKE	LIZARD	SALAMANDER
Reptile	Reptile	Amphibian
Dry skin covered with scales; Underside has one row of single scales	Dry skin made up of scales	Smooth, moist skin
No legs	Most have four legs; Some have two legs; A few have no legs	Most have four legs; Some have two legs; A few have no legs
	Five toes on each foot; Toes have claws	Four toes on front feet; Five toes on hind feet; Toes have no claws
No eardrums	Eardrums visible on head; Most have eyelids	No eardrums; Most have eyelids

SNAKE

Females lay eggs with
leathery shells on land
or give birth to live young

Young and old breathe
with lungs

Cannot grow a new tail

LIZARD

Females lay eggs with
leathery shells on land or give
birth to live young;
Babies look like
miniature adults

Young and old breathe
with lungs

Most can grow a new tail

SALAMANDER

Females lay soft, jellylike
eggs in water;
Babies live in
water and breathe
with gills

Adults breathe with lungs

Can grow new tail, legs, or feet

Naturalist John Hanson Mitchell says there is one rule that helps you know a lizard
from a salamander: "If you can catch it, it is a salamander; if you can't, it's a lizard."
(From *A Field Guide to Your Own Back Yard*, W. W. Norton & Co., NY: 1985.)

Also by Margery Facklam:

Spiders and Their Web Sites

Creepy, Crawly Caterpillars

The Big Bug Book

*In joyous memory of Howard Facklam,
who loved all wildlife, including lizards*

—M.F.

Text copyright © 2003 by Margery Facklam
Illustrations copyright © 2003 by Alan Male

First Edition

Library of Congress Cataloging-in-Publication Data

Facklam, Margery.
    Lizards: weird and wonderful / by Margery Facklam ; illustrated by Alan Male — 1st ed.
        p. cm.
    ISBN 0-316-17346-0
        1. Lizards. I. Male, Alan. II. Title.

QL666.L2 F23 2003
597.9'5—dc21   2002019173

10 9 8 7 6 5 4 3 2 1

TWP

Printed in Singapore